BOURBON-ORLÉANS

A Family Album

Prince Michael of Greece

Cover pictures:

The photographs on the front and back covers were taken in the park of Orleans House, the English residence of the duc d'Aumale. He had commissioned them as part of an album which was sold for charity. On the back cover he is shown holding one column of the gazebo surrounded by members of his family and Court. The picture on the inside of the cover was taken in England in 1866 and shows most of the Orléans family gathered for the funeral of Queen Marie Amélie.

Published by

ROSVALL
Royal Books

Enasen – Falekvarna
521 91 FALKÖPING, Sweden
tel: 46-515-37105 fax: 46-515-37165
email: royalbooks@telia.com

ISBN 91-975671-4-0
Elanders, Falköping 2009

Prince Michael of Greece

H.R.H. Prince Michael of Greece and Denmark was born in Rome in 1939, the only child of Prince Christopher of Greece and his second wife, Princess Françoise of France. On his father's side he is related to practically all the Orthodox and Protestant Royal houses of Europe, including Greece, Denmark, Norway, Russia, England and Romania and to most German dynasties. On his mother's side he is related to all the Catholic houses, including France, Belgium, Luxemburg, Spain, Portugal, Italy, Brazil and Austria.

Prince Michael is an author and historian, who has published a number of essays, biographies and historical novels, including *Le Vol du Régent, Le Rajah Bourbon, Les Joyaux des Tsars, Le Dernier Sultan, Louis XIV: L'Envers du Soleil, Joyaux de Couronnes d'Europe, Imperial Palaces of Russia* and many others.

In 1965, Prince Michael married Marina Karella, a renowned artist and sculptress. The couple now divide their time been their homes in Paris and Greece. They have two daughters and three grandchildren.

Princess Françoise of France

Introduction

The royal House of France had its roots in the 9th century. Profiting from the decadence of the Merovingian kingdom, the family carved a small principality for themselves around a tiny city with the name of Paris. In 987, one of their number, Hugues Capet, was elected king. The nobles chose him because he was the weakest, the least important and the least capable of annoying them. Through generation after generation his descendants had two aims: to transform the elective monarchy into a hereditary monarchy for their family and to enlarge their territories by marriage and inheritance rather than by war. They succeeded in making France the most important power in Europe and a beacon of European civilisation. For nearly 1000 years the same dynasty ruled, making the House of France the oldest European Royal family, sharing with the Serbian reigning family the unusual distinction of being native to their own country; every other European dynasty was imported. Down the ages different branches of the House of France occupied the throne one after the other: the Capetians, the Valois, the Valois-Angoulêmes, the Bourbons and finally the Orléans.

The Orléans branch started with Louis XIV's brother Philippe de France, duc d'Orléans. Brilliant, talented, charming, unconventional, scandalous and daring, his descendants were lovers of art who were also noted for their political ambitions. The most famous of them were the son of Philippe de France, Philippe, duc d'Orléans, who ruled as Regent during Louis XV's minority; the infamous Philippe Egalité, who became an extreme left wing revolutionary and King Louis Philippe, who remained one of the most successful rulers in the history of his country.

Since the extinction of the eldest branch of the French Bourbons, the Orléans have been, and still are, the only rightful heirs to the crown of France. My mother Princess Françoise was one of the family, a daughter of the duc de Guise and a sister of the Count of Paris, Henri VI. She married Prince Christopher of Greece, son of King George I and Grand Duchess Olga of Russia. This was one of the then very rare marriages between a Roman Catholic and a non-Catholic, my father being Orthodox. I am the sole product of that union.

Prince Michael of Greece

LOUIS PHILIPPE I
King of the French 1830-1848
1773-1850 m1809
MARIE AMÉLIE THÉRÈSE
Princess of The Two Sicilies 1782-1866

Ferdinand, Duke of Orleans
1810-1842 m1837 **Hélène**
of Mecklenburg-Schwerin 1814-1858

- **Philippe, Count of Paris**
  1838-1894 m1864
  Isabella, Infanta of Spain 1848-1919

- **Robert, Duke of Chartres**
  1840-1910 m1863
  Francois of Orléans 1844-1925

Louise
1812-1850 m1832 **Léopold I,**
King of the Belgians 1790-1865

- **Léopold of Belgium** 1833-1834

- **Léopold II of Belgium** 1835-1909 m1853
  Marie Henriette of Austria 1836-1902

- **Philippe, Count of Flanders** 1837-1905
  m1867 **Marie of Hohenzollern** 1845-1912

- **Charlotte of Belgium** 1840-1927 m1857
  Maximilian I of Mexico 1832-1867

Marie
1813-1850 m1832 **Alexander**
of Württemberg 1804-1881

- **Philipp of Württemberg**
  1838-1917 m1865
  Maria Theresia of Austria
  1845-1927

Louis, Duke of Nemours
1814-1896 m1840 **Victoire of**
Saxe-Coburg and Gotha 1822-1857

- **Gaston, Comte of Eu**
  1842-1922 m1864 **Isabel,**
  Princess Imperial of Brazil 1846-1921

- **Ferdinand, Duke of Alencon**
  1844-1910 m1868
  Sophie, Duchess in Bavaria 1847-1897

- **Marguerite of Orléans** 1846-1893
  m1872 **Wladyslaw Czartoryski** 1828-1894

- **Blanche of Orléans** 1857-1943

Francoise
1816-1818

Clémentine
1817-1907 m1843 **August**
of Saxe-Coburg 1818-1881

- **Philipp of Saxe-Coburg** 1844-1921
  m1875 **Louise of Belgium** 1858-1924

- **August of Saxe-Coburg** 1845-1907
  m1864 **Leopoldina of Brazil** 1847-1871

- **Clotilde of Saxe-Coburg** 1846-1927
  m1864 **Joseph of Austria** 1833-1905

- **Amalie of Saxe-Coburg** 1848-1894 m1875
  Max Emanuel, Duke in Bavaria 1849-1893

- **Ferdinand, King of Bulgaria** 1861-1848
  m1893 **Marie Louise of Parma** 1870-1899
  m1908 **Eleonore of Reuss** 1860-1917

Francois, Prince of Joinville
1818-1900 m1843 Francoise
of Brazil 1824-1898

- **Francoise of Orléans**
  1844-1925 m1863
  Robert, Duke of Chartres
  1840-1910

- **Pierre, Duke of Penthièvre**
  1845-1919

- son 1849

Charles
1820-1828

Henri, Duke of Aumale
1822-1897 m1844 **Marie Caroline**
of The Two Sicilies 1822-1869

- **Louis Philippe, Prince of Condé**
  1846-1866

- **Henri, Duke of Guise** 1847-1847

- **Francois, Duke of Guise** 1852-1852

- **Francois Louis, Duke of Guise**
  1854-1872

Antoine, Duke of Montpensier
1824-1890 m1846 **Luisa Fernanda,**
Infanta of Spain 1832-1897

- **Infanta Isabella** 1848-1919 m1864
  Philippe, Count of Paris 1838-1894

- **Infanta Maria Amélia** 1851-1870

- **Infanta Maria Christina** 1852-1879

- **Infanta Maria dela Regla** 1856-1861

- **Infante Fernando** 1859-1873

- **Infanta Maria de las Mercedes** 1860-1878
  m1878 **Alfonso XII, King of Spain**

- **Infante Felipe** 1862-1864

- **Infante Antonio** 1866-1930 m1886
  Infanta Eulalia of Spain 1864-1958

King Louis Philippe of France and his wife Queen Marie Amélie. He was the son of the Duke of Orléans who became known as citizen "Egalité" during the French Revolution, and voted for the death of his cousin Louis XVI. Louis Philippe himself had fought in the revolutionary armies. From 1830 to 1848, he ruled France and gave to his country 18 years of prosperity and peace. He was dethroned by a short revolution and died in exile in England. His wife was the daughter of King Ferdinand I of the Two Sicilies and the famous Queen Maria Carolina, sister of Marie Antoinette. Louis Philippe and Marie Amélie were an exception in the history of the House of Orléans, being a loving, devoted and faithful couple.

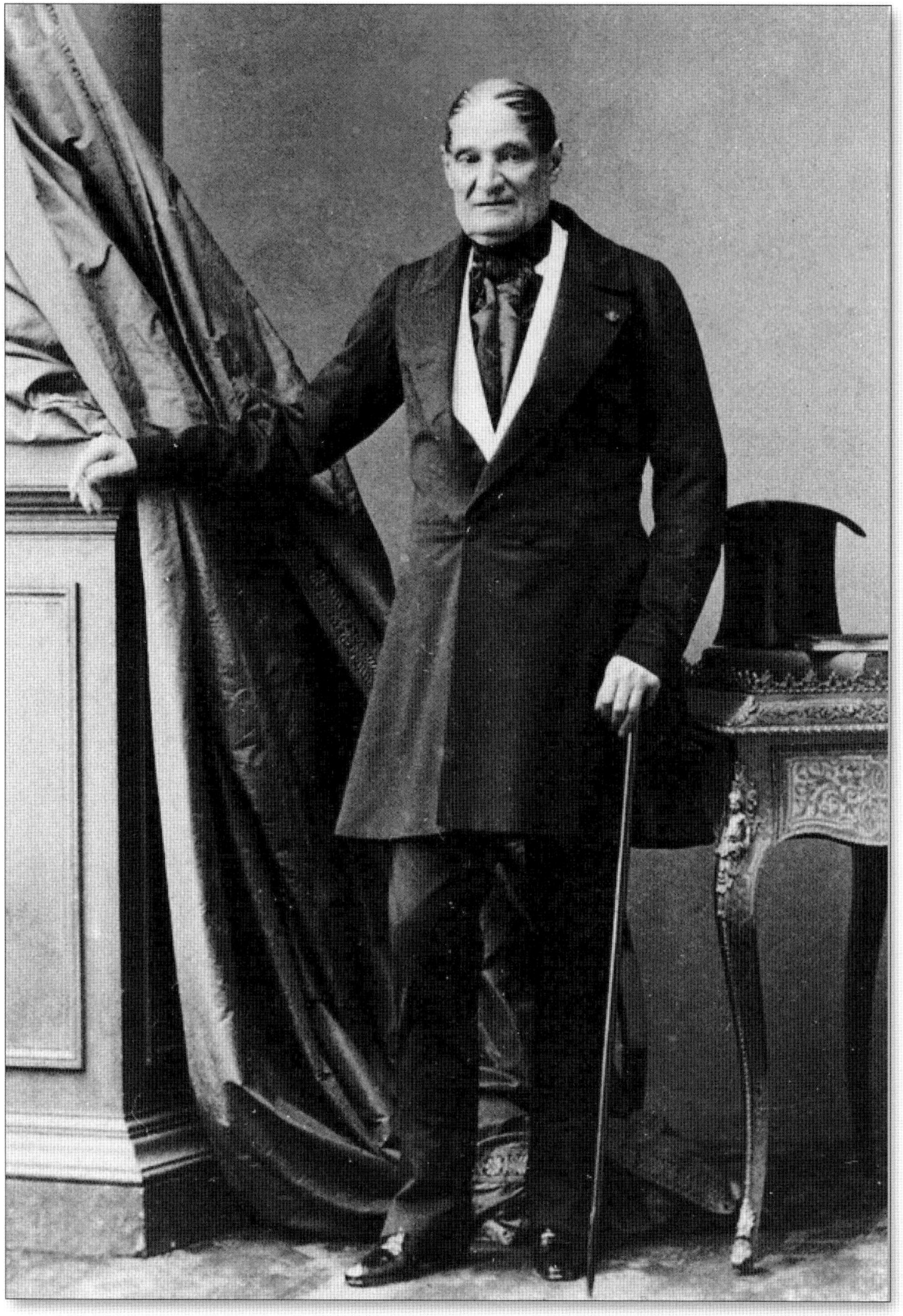

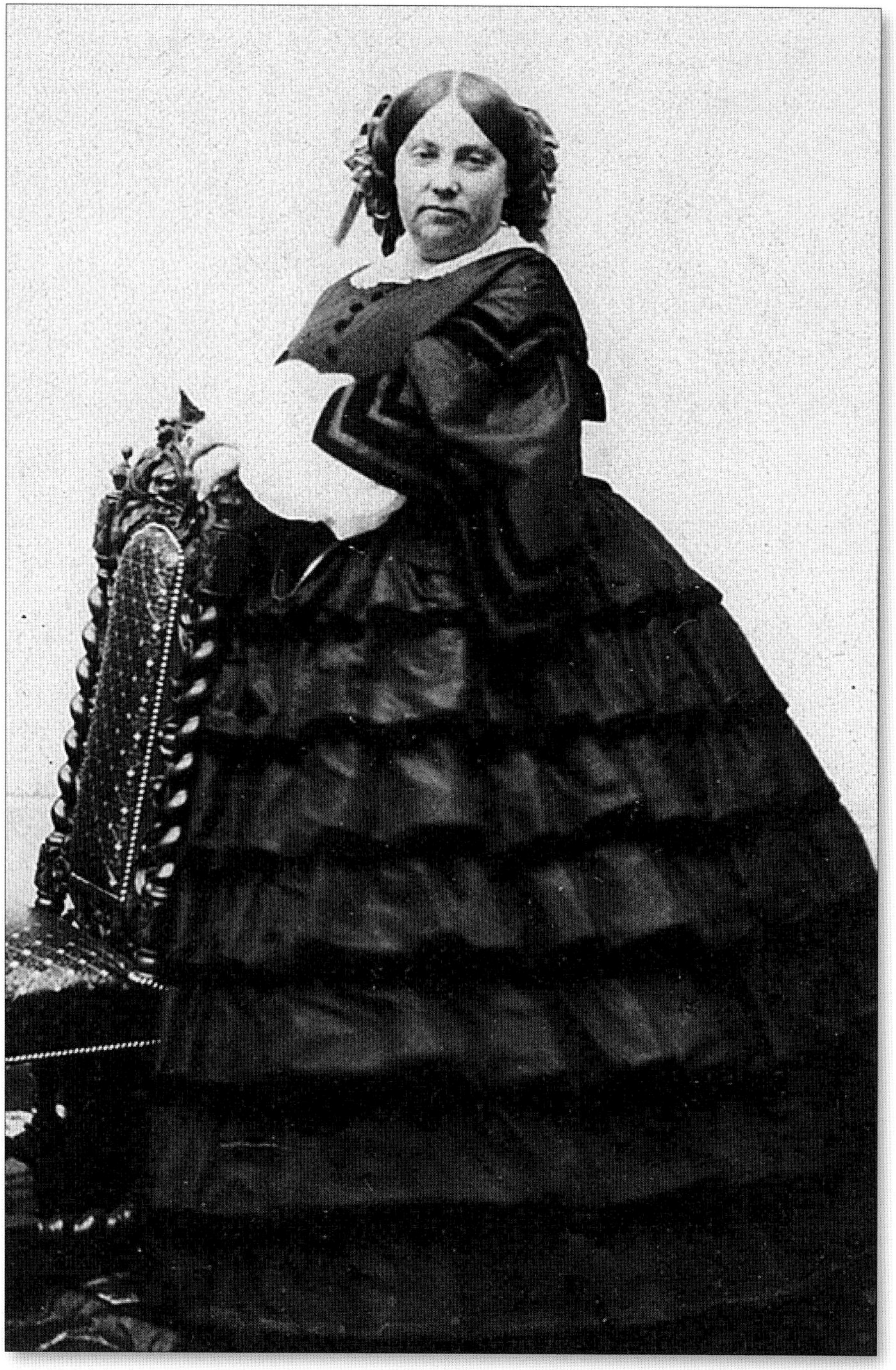

Left: Madame Royale, Princess Marie Thérèse Charlotte of France, the only surviving child of Louis XVI and Marie Antoinette. She married her 1st cousin, the Duke of Angoulême and returned to France in 1815. Exiled again in 1830 she lived the rest of her life in Edinburgh, Prague, Gorizia and finally in Austria. She died at Frohsdorf in 1851. Marie-Thérèse is described on her gravestone as the Queen Dowager of France, a reference to her husband's twenty-minute rule as King Louis XIX of France. Right: Maria Theresa of Modena, the wife of the Count of Chambord.

At the time Louis Philippe was ruling, there were still survivors of the Napoleonic past, like the Emperor's youngest brother Jerome (extreme left). There were also living members of the eldest branch of the Bourbons that the revolution of 1830 had sent in exile, like the niece, see above, and grand-children of King Charles X, the Mademoiselle of Artois, Duchess of Parma (left) and her brother, the Count of Chambord (right)

(Left) Another photo of Queen Marie Amélie, the beloved matriarch of the Orléans family in her old age in exile in Claremont, where Queen Victoria allowed the family to live. Thanks to King Louis Philippe, their elder daughter Louise made a brilliant marriage with Prince Leopold of Saxe-Coburg-Gotha, the newly elected King of the Belgians (both painted here by Winterhalter). He was the widower of the heiress of the British throne, Charlotte, Princess of Wales. Louise of Belgium became extremely popular in Belgium and died of consumption while still very young.

Her elder son Leopold II (right) succeeded his father Leopold I. He was known for his love of money and notorious for the brutality with which he carved and ruled the Congo, his African colony. He married Archduchess Maria Henrietta of Austria (far right). Both are represented in 17th century costumes for a costume ball. This photograph of Leopold II in a costume similar to that worn by his ancestor Louis XIV is unique

The eldest daughter of Leopold II, Princess Louise of Belgium, married her father's first cousin, Prince Philippe of Saxe-Coburg, son of Clementine d'Orléans. He was one of the few witnesses of the drama at Mayerling, where Archduke Rudolph of Austria and his mistress Marie Vetsera died. He was also a difficult man and his marriage with Louise was unhappy. Finally she eloped with a Hungarian Count, with the result that she was ostracised afterwards by all royal families: her later life was miserable.

Stephanie of Belgium, the second daughter of Leopold II, was married to Archduke Rudolph, heir of the Austro-Hungarian Empire. It was another unhappy marriage. Eleven years after Rudolph's death at Mayerling, Stephanie married the Hungarian Count Elemér Lónyay de Nagy-Lónya et Vásáros-Namény, who was later elevated to the title of Prince.

Clémentine of Belgium, the last daughter of Leopold II, was luckier than her sisters. She fell in love with the heir of Napoleon, Prince Victor Napoleon, (right) the head of the imperial House of France. Her father was outraged by the idea that his daughter might marry the descendant of the "usurper" so Clémentine wisely waited until her father's death. Then she quietly married her beloved. Thanks to her, the blood of the French royal house is mixed with the blood of relatives of the "Corsican adventurer".

Ferdinand of Orléans was the eldest of the children of Louis Philippe and Marie Amélie, and was originally given the title Duke of Chartres. When his father became King of the French, it was however changed to "Duke of Orléans". In 1837 he married Hélène of Mecklenburg-Schwerin, who was and remained a protestant. Their two sons, Philippe and Robert were born in 1838 and 1840. Two years later, Ferdinand was killed in a carriage accident at Neuilly.

The dowager Duchess of Orléans, Hélène of Mecklenburg-Schwerin, with her two sons in around 1845. After 1848 she lived in exile mostly in Germany and died in 1857 at Richmond in Surrey. Painting by Winterhalter.

Marie of Orléans, a daughter of Louis Philippe and Marie Amélie, married Prince Alexander of Württemberg. It was not a grand marriage. Marie was a brilliantly gifted sculptor and like her sister Louise died very young of consumption. Both she and her husband are painted here by Winterhalter.

Philipp, Duke of Württemberg, Marie's only child, with his wife Maria Theresia of Austria and their two eldest children, the twins Albrecht and Marie Amalie. Albrecht is the grandfather of the present Duke of Württemberg, who is married to Princess Diane of France

The Duke of Nemours, Louis d'Orléans, was the second son of Louis Philippe. He was the least brilliant of his brothers and never succeeded in beoming popular. Nevertheless, he was a good soldier like his brothers and the essence of dignity. He married Princess Victoria of Saxe-Coburg, the favourite cousin of Queen Victoria. They had two sons. The elder, Gaston d'Orléans, Count of Eu, was sent to Brazil in order to marry the youngest daughter of the Brazilian Emperor, but the eldest, Isabelle, fell in love with him and he married her instead [right].

Above left: Princess Marguerite of Orléans, the elder daughter of The Duke of Nemours. She later married the Polish Prince Czartoryski.
Below left: The Duke of Nemours as an old man with his unmarried daughter, Princess Blanche of Orléans, at the opening of a charity bazaar.

The Brazilian princesses were the daughters of Emperor Pedro II. He was an extraordinary character, a liberal, an intellectual, a friend of Victor Hugo and Darwin. He abolished slavery in Brazil and so was dethroned by the great landlords, a reverse of fortune he accepted philosophically. He died in exile in France. He married Princess Teresa Christina of Bourbon-Two-Sicilies (left). The eldest daughter, Isabella (right), Crown Princess of Brazil, was the wife of the Count of Eu and they founded the House of Orléans-Bragance, a Brazilian branch of the House of France. Isabella is shown here with their eldest son, Prince Pedro.

The imperial family of Brazil. This picture shows the simplicity of the Court at Rio de Janeiro. The emperor is standing next to his wife, Empress Teresa Christina. Next to her is the widower of her second daughter, a Prince of Saxe-Coburg-Gotha. On the left of the picture, the Count and Countess of Eu with their three sons. The Countess of Eu was also Crown Princess of Brazil. Right: The Count and Countess of Eu with their three sons, Pedro, Luiz and Antonio.

The imperial family of Brazil in exile in France during the First World War, in front of the Château d'Eu. The count and countess of Eu are recognizable in front of their three sons, Princes Luiz, Antoine and Pedro. In front of Prince Pedro is his wife, Princess Elisabeth and between her and the coount of Eu is young Princess Isabella of Orléans-Braganza, the future Countess of Paris. On the extreme left is Princess Luiz of Orléans-Braganza, born Maria Pia of Bourbon-Sicily, with her own children. The two Princes Louis and Antoine wear British uniform: as members of the former reigning family of France they were not allowed to fight in the French army.

Duchess Sophie in Bavaria, Duchess of Alençon

The brother of the count of Eu was Ferdinand of Orléans, Duke of Alençon. He was allowed to serve in the Spanish army and is shown here in Spanish uniform. He married Duchess Sophie in Bavaria, a sister of Empress Elizabeth of Austria and Queen Maria of Naples. Sophie was betrothed first to her cousin, King Ludwig II of Bavaria, but he broke the engagement without giving any reason. Her family was furious. No one knows if she found happiness with the Duke of Alençon.

Another picture of Sophie, Duchess of Alençon (right), who had very long hair like her sister the Empress of Austria. Sophie died in a frightful accident. She was the leading figure in a charitable event called "Le bazar de la Charité" in Paris. When the building caught fire, she was burnt alive while trying to save other people. The shock was immense for all her relatives and particularly for her husband. They had two children, a son Emanuel and a daughter (above left), Louise of Orléans, who married a distant relative on her mother's side, Prince Alfons of Bavaria.

The Duke of Alençon in later years.

The son of the Duke of Alençon and Sophie of Bavaria was Emmanuel of Orléans, Duke of Vendôme. He made a brilliant union, marrying Princess Henriette, a sister of King Albert I of Belgium. She was a talented painter and writer with all the Christian virtues. They had four children. In the 1930s they lost a lot of money and had to sell the fabulous treasures they had inherited from the House of Orléans.

The Duke and Duchess of Vendôme with their three elder children, Louise, Sophie and Geneviève. A son, Charles, was born in 1905.

*As founder of a new dynasty Ferdinand quickly took a wife, marrying Princess Marie Louise of Bourbon Parma and had four children.
Below: Ferdinand's elder children: Boris, Cyrill and Eudoxie*

Far left: Clémentine of Orléans was the youngest daughter of King Louis Philippe and inherited the family genius for political intrigue. She married Prince August of Saxe-Coburg who had an immense fortune from his Hungarian mother. Clémentine transformed her Viennese residence, the Palais Coburg, into the centre of a vast spider's web. She knew everything, her influence was widespread; she even managed to put her younger son Ferdinand (left and right) on the throne of Bulgaria. At the beginning, there were few people in Europe who wanted Ferdinand to be ruler of Bulgaria. Yet, with a genius equal to his mother's, he managed to be recognized by all the Powers and to transform the undeveloped country into a modern state. Right: Clémentine when old.

François of Orléans, Prince of Joinville (above) was the most charming of Louis Philippe's sons. It was during one of his long voyages that he landed in Rio de Janeiro, and it was there that he fell in love with Princess Francisca (right), a daughter of Pedro I of Brazil, and married her. The couple had a daughter, Francoise, and one son, Pierre of Orléans, Duke of Penthièvre. The Prince of Joinville was also an extraordinarily talented painter whose watercolours recorded every event of his adventurous life.

Far right: Francisca, Princess of Joinville, shown with her only daughter, Françoise of Orleans, Duchess of Chartres, her granddaughter Marie of Orléans, Princess Valdemar of Denmark, and her great-grandson, Prince Aage of Denmark

Left: The Duke of Penthièvre. He was a sailor and fell in love with a lady of unequal birth, whom the rules of his family forbade him to marry. She gave him various children but he was ostracized by the Orléans family and was rarely seen in public.

25

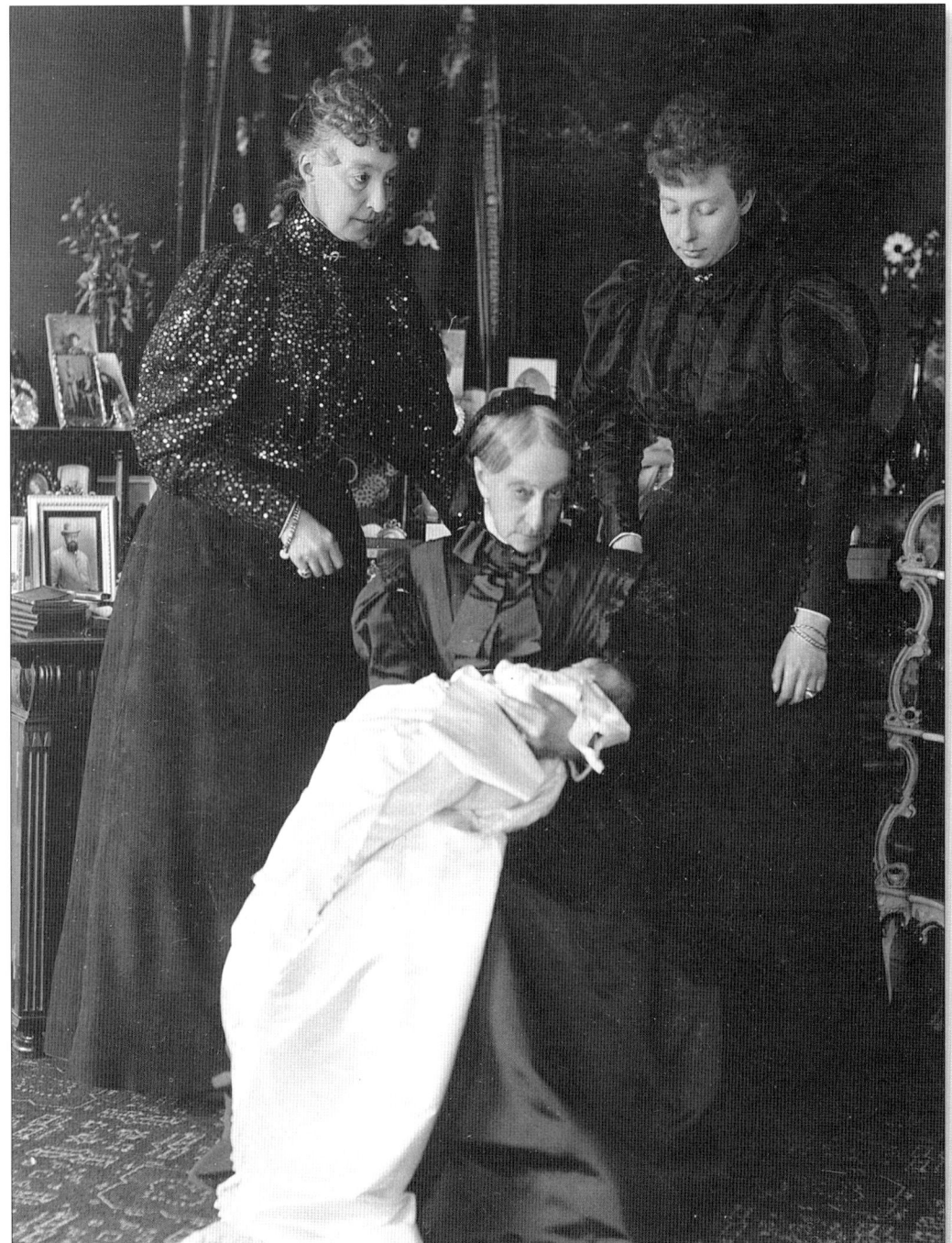

26

The Duke of Aumale had his nephews and nieces photographed by the best artists (above). He had four sons of his own, but not one survived adolescence so he died childless, believing he was subject to a curse. After the death of his wife, he chose as his constant companion a very distinguished and dignified lady named Countess Berthe of Clinchamp. She acted as a discreet hostess in Chantilly and rumour said that the Duke of Aumale married her secretly before he died. (right).

Henri of Orleans, Duke of Aumale (left) was the most famous son of King Louis Philippe. Through rather sinister circumstances he inherited the fabulous fortune of the princes of Condé, which made him one of the richest men in Europe. He became an avid collector, transforming his splendid Château of Chantilly into a treasure house. He was also a remarkable soldier, master-minding the conquest of Algeria, he was a gifted politician, and finally he was a successful womaniser. Yet he always remained in love with his wife, Princess Maria Carolina of Bourbon-Sicily (far left). She was also his cousin, belonging to the same royal house as his mother, Queen Marie Amélie.

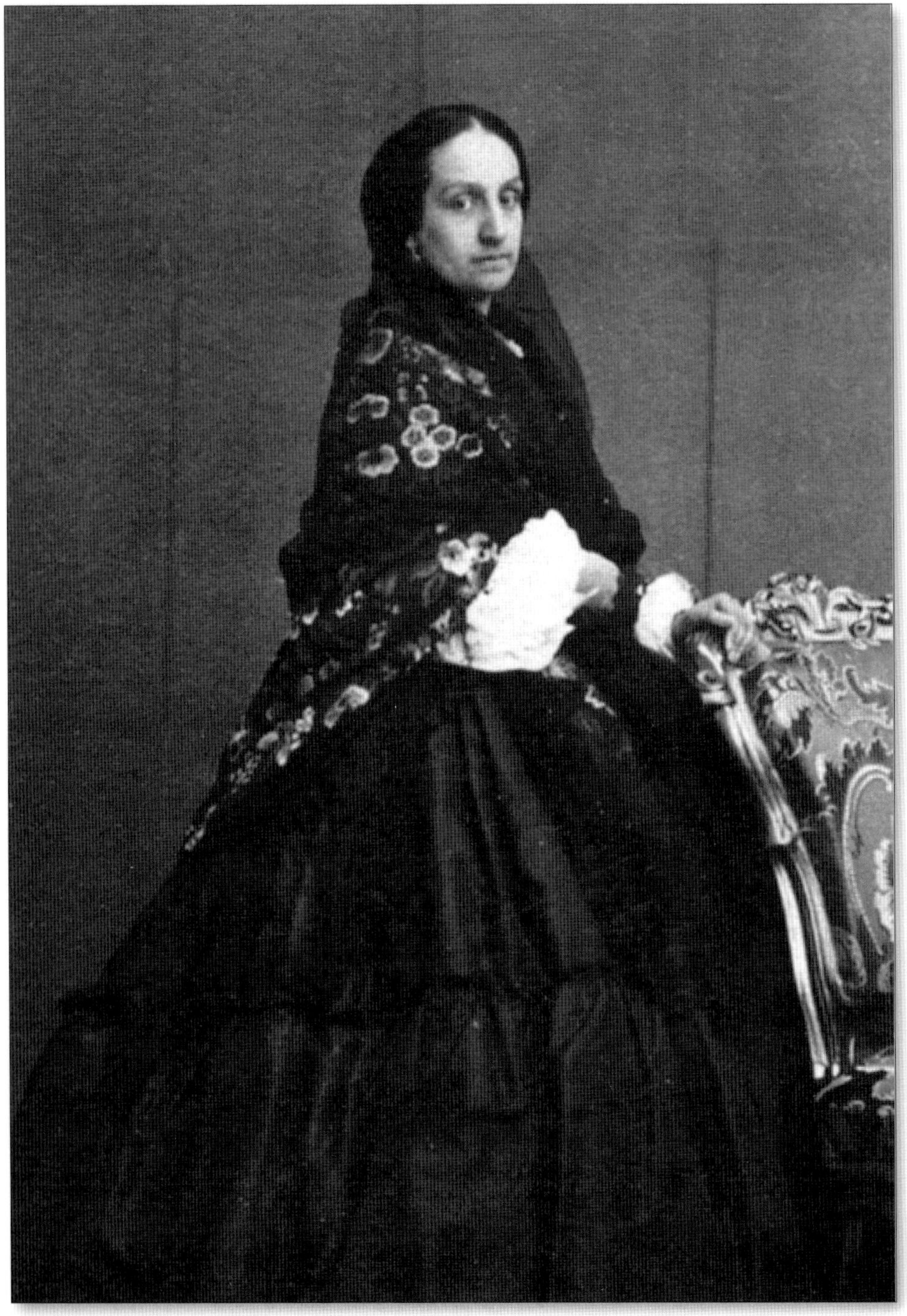

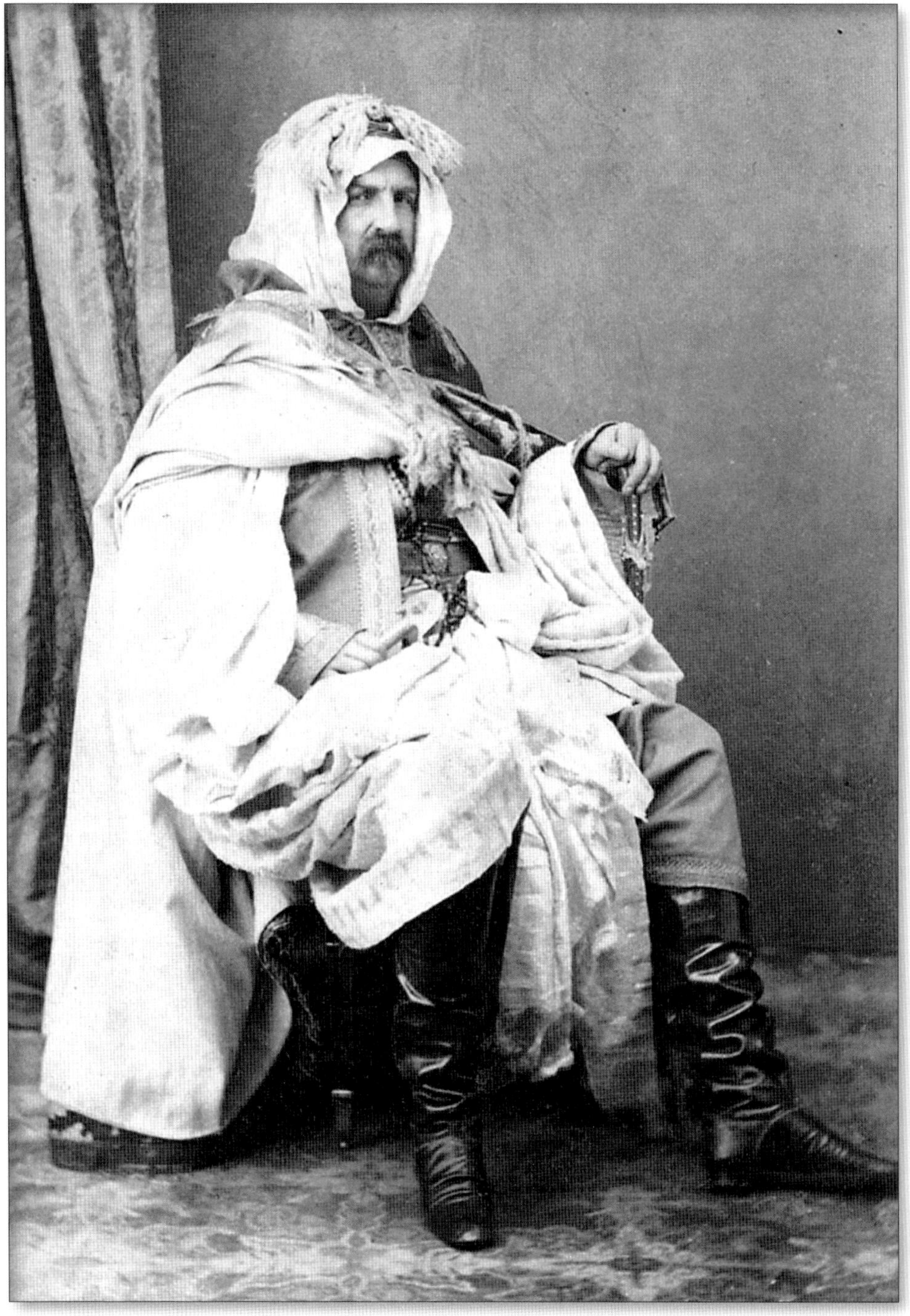

The Duke of Montpensier and his daughter, Infanta Isabelle, who was to marry her first cousin the Count of Paris, heir of King Louis Philippe. Right: Antoine of Orléans, the son of the Duke of Montpensier, was made Duke of Galliera when he inherited the enormous fortune of a Genoese widow, the Duchess of Galliera. He led a rather useless and scandalous life.

Left: Antoine of Orleans, Duke of Montpensier, dressed here as an Arab sheikh for a costume ball, was a tireless intriguer. He married Infanta Maria Louisa Fernanda of Spain (far left), only sister of the reigning Queen Isabella II. The unscrupulous Montpensier tried to overthrow his sister-in-law to become King of Spain himself. For this he was exiled to Seville, then a sleepy forgotten town which he transformed, modernised and made into one of the most brilliant cities of Spain. He founded the Spanish branch of the Orléans family, which survives to this day.

The Duke of Montpensier was the son-in-law of the Queen Regent of Spain, Maria Christina of Bourbon-Two-Sicilies (left), widow of Ferdinand VII. She was beautiful and rather shameless in keeping a lover, Munos, giving him many children and making him a duke. But she also strove with courage and panache to preserve the throne of her daughter Isabella II (centre). Isabella was a formidable character; she was ugly, intelligent, extremely brave, rather cynical and unafraid of scandal. She tried to rule despite a civil war that was launched by her uncle Don Carlos. Finally she was deposed and spent many years in exile in Paris. After much upheaval in Spain her son Alfonso XII (right) ascended to the throne. Peace was restored, Spaniards rallied around the young King and the future seemed promising: then Alfonso XII unexpectedly died.

Just after he ascended the throne, young Alfonso XII fell in love with the only princess his mother did not approve of, his first cousin, Infanta Mercedes d'Orléans (left), a daughter of the Duke of Montpensier who had intrigued so much against Queen Isabella. Yet, love won in the end. Isabella and her sister, the Infanta Maria Luisa Fernanda, Duchess of Montpensier, were reconciled and their children married. Everyone was happy. Yet, a few months later Queen Mercedes died of consumption. Alfonso XII was devastated but he had to remarry in order to produce an heir. He chose Archduchess Maria Christina of Austria (centre). Not long after, he himself died leaving no son, though his Queen was pregnant. Spain had to wait a few months to see who the next ruler would be. Then a son was born who became King of Spain at the moment of birth under the name Alfonso XIII (right, with his nanny). Queen Maria Christina was appointed regent. She ruled with an extraordinary sense of duty and great dignity, but she could not prevail Spain from losing its colonial empire through war with United States.

Isabella, Countess of Paris, wearing the famous parure of sapphires and diamonds which, according to the legend, first belonged to Queen Marie Antoinette, then to Empress Josephine who left it to her daughter Queen Hortense, from whom Louis Philippe bought it.

Infanta Maria Louisa Fernanda, widow of the Duke of Montpensier, with her only surviving daughter, Infanta Isabella, Countess of Paris. The décor of a gothic window is typical of the photographic art of the day.

Infanta Eulalia

The only surviving son of the Infanta Maria Louisa and the Duke of Montpensier, Antoine of Orléans, Duke of Galliera, married his first cousin Infanta Eulalia, daughter of Isabella II. Eulalia was beautiful and knew it. She was also extraordinarily outspoken, especially in her memoirs. She was a great personality, who outlived all her relatives.

1896

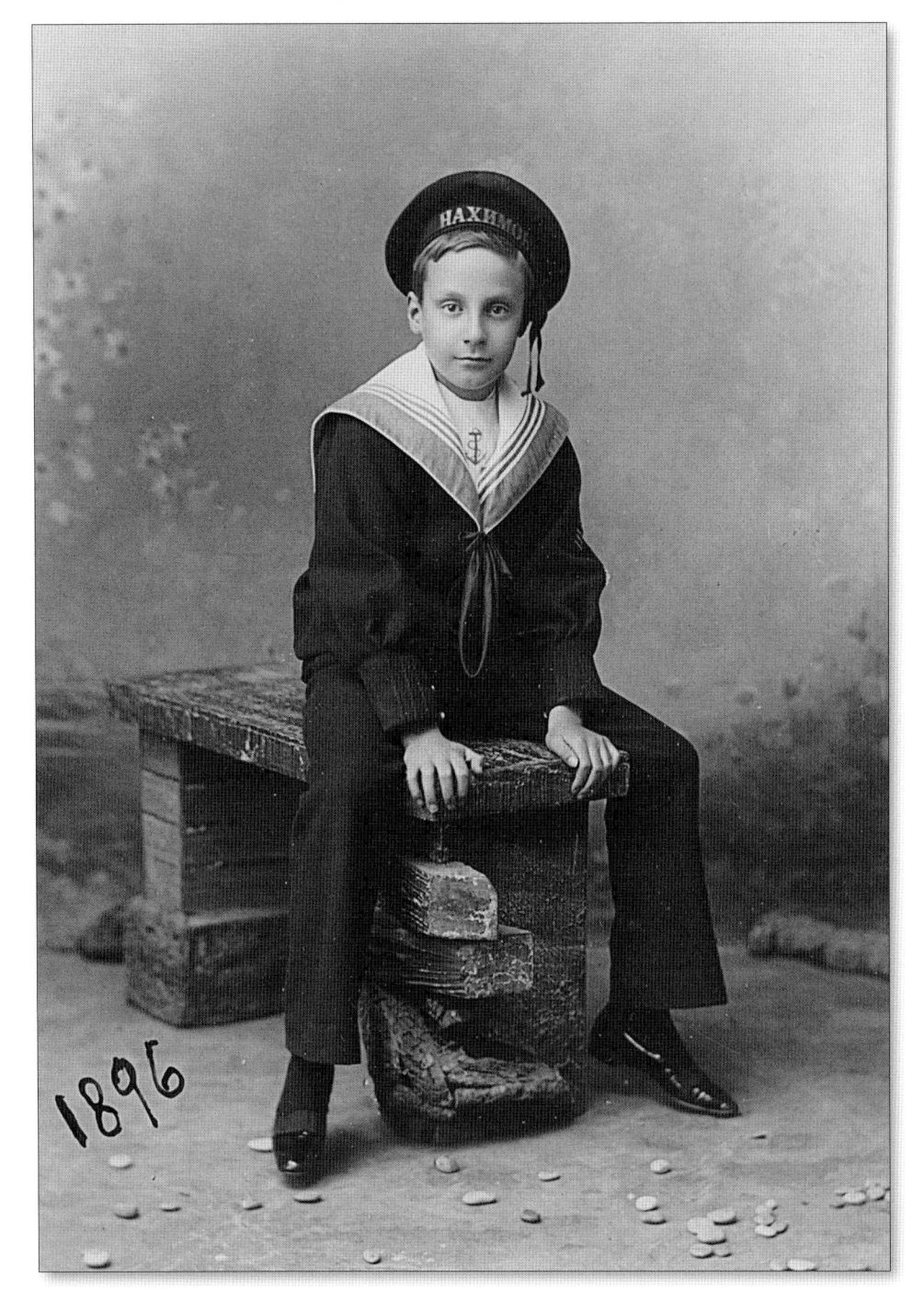

1896

34

Infante Don Alfonso of Orléans and Bourbon married Princess Beatrice of Edinburgh and Saxe-Coburg, one of the beautiful daughters of Prince Alfred, Duke of Edinburgh. Beside her is her sister Alexandra of Hohenlohe-Langenburg, then their mother Grand Duchess Maria Alexandrovna of Russia and Prince Leopold of Battenberg.

The two sons of the Duke of Galliera and Infanta Eulalia. Far left: Infante Alfonso of Orléans and Bourbon. He was a formidable character: a famous pilot and very eccentric. His brother Infante Don Luis (left), meanwhile, was at the centre of so many scandals that his titles and decorations were taken from him.

36

Infanta Isabella of Spain, eldest daughter of Queen Isabella II (right). Infanta Isabella married her mother's 1st cousin, Prince Gaetano of The Two Sicilies, who died after only three years of marriage. Isabella, who at one point was the Princess of Asturias (Crown Princess), was a central figure at the Spanish court.

Right: Queen Isabella II with her husband, who was also her cousin, Infante Francisco de Assis of Spain. The marriage was arranged for political reasons, mainly by France. It was very unhappy, the two consorts had practically nothing in common. Many rumours circulated about the private life of the Queen and the King Consort.

Left: Queen Isabella II of Spain on a visit to her niece, Infanta Isabella, Countess of Paris (left), accompanied by her courtiers (behind the Queen is her lady-in-waiting the Duchess of Villa Hermosa). The Count of Paris is standing behind the table; next to him is his daughter Princess Hélène of France.

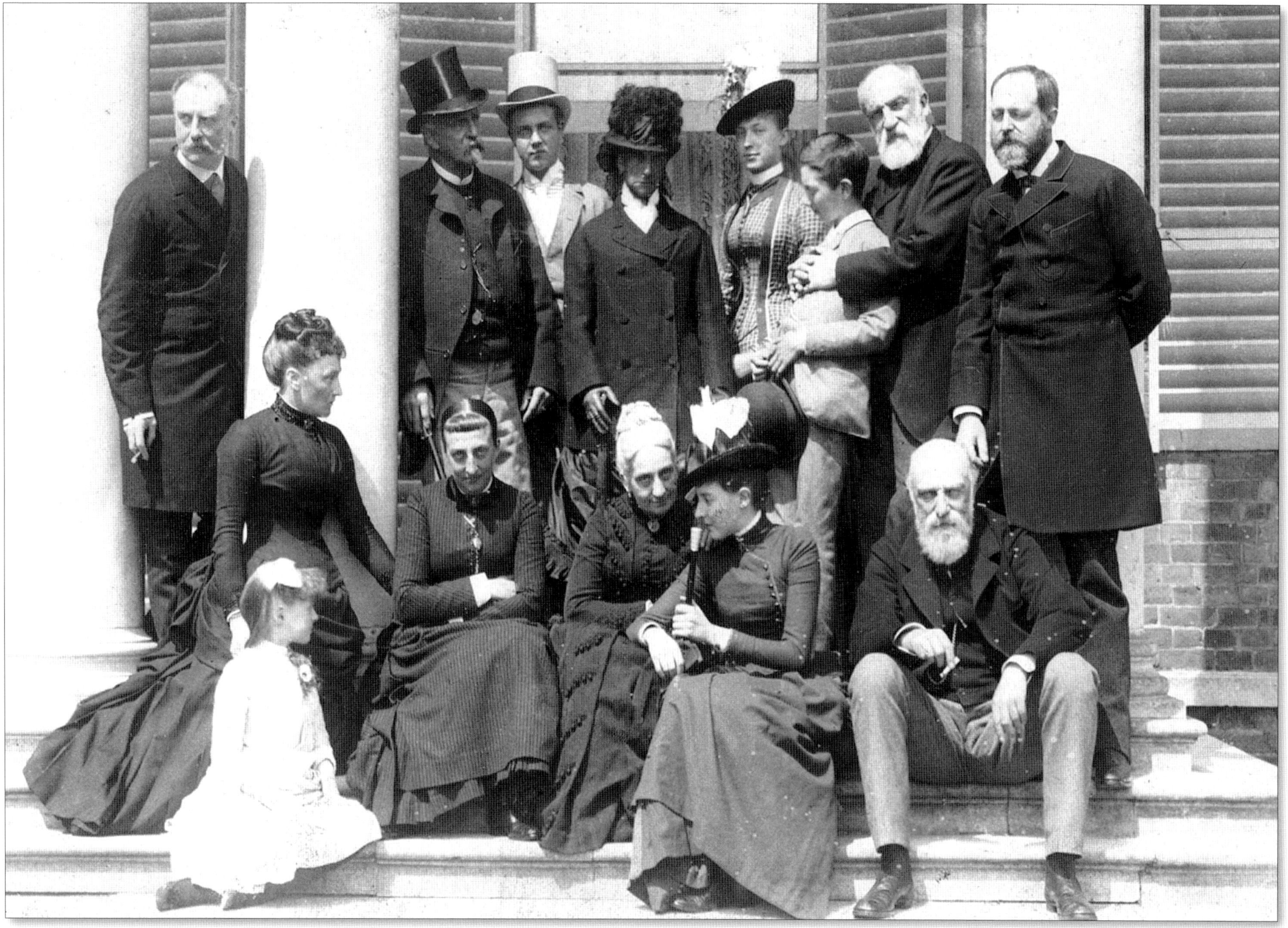

The Prince of Wales (later Edward VII) pays a courtesy visit to Philippe, Duke of Orleans at Stowe House at the time of the death of the Duke's father, the Count of Paris. Roght: The Countess of Paris in mourning with three of her daughters, Isabelle, Duchess of Guise, Hélène, Duchess of Aosta and Louise, Infanta of Spain.

Left: An extraordinary image showing many members of the House of Orléans together, including three surviving sons of King Louis Philippe. (Back row): unknown, The Duke of Aumale, Prince Henri of Orléans, The Princess of Joinville, Princess Marguerite of Orléans, Prince Jean of Orléans, The Prince of Joinville, The Count of Paris. (In front, left to right) : unknown, unknown, The Countess of Paris, The Duchess of Montpensier, Princess Hélène of Orléans, The Duke of Montpensier.

Every year, the Count of Paris, then in exile in England, and his family used to go to Scotland in the hunting season. The Countess of Paris (above) shot like a man. She is known to have been out riding in the country when pregnant and to have shot six birds, before returning home to give birth to her last child, Ferdinand, Duke of Montpensier: then she had the six birds cooked and ate them.

The children of the Count and Countess of Paris followed their parents to Scotland and were dressed like little Highlanders. (From left to right) Princesses Isabelle and Louise and Prince Ferdinand.

Philippe, Duke of Orléans, elder son of the Count and Countess of Paris. He was handsome and had great success with ladies. In trying to keep him far from his conquests, he was packed off to Russia. But his parents' plan was unsuccessful and he had many amorous adventures in Saint Petersburg and Moscow. He is here shown in the uniform of a Tartar soldier.

Philippe's younger brother Ferdinand of Orléans, Duke of Montpensier. Unlike his blue-eyed brother and sisters, Ferdinand inherited the dark eyes of his grandmother the Infanta.

The bridegroom Don Carlos was the son of the eccentric red-haired Queen of Portugal, Maria Pia of Savoy. The child is her eldest grandson, Prince Luiz Filipe.

The eldest daughter of the Count and Countess of Paris, Princess Amélie, married the Crown Prince of Portugal, Don Carlos of Braganza. The reception that the Count of Paris gave in Paris on the occasion of her wedding was so brilliant and so well-attended that the republican Parliament took fright at the thought of a possible return of the monarchy and sent him into exile.

Queen Amélie of Portugal in Court dress. She is wearing a splendid emerald and diamond necklace and a tiara made of diamond stars which are still preserved in Lisbon. An imposing figure, Queen Amélie was also extremely good-hearted. Her husband King Carlos became enormously fat. He was a very good amateur painter, loved women and became slightly bored with his wife.

Queen Amélie and King Carlos in the royal carriage. They were seated exactly like this with their two sons one day when an anarchist approached the carriage and shot the King and their eldest son Prince Luiz Filipe, killing them both. He missed the second son, Dom Manuel, because Queen Amélie threw her bouquet of flowers in his face.

King Carlos and Queen Amélie following the Corpus Christi procession in the streets of Lisbon.

The two sons of King Carlos and Queen Amelia, Prince Luiz Filipe (left), who would be murdered with his father, and (right) Prince Manuel, who on the death of his father and elder brother became King Manuel II.

45

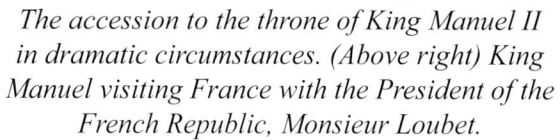

The accession to the throne of King Manuel II in dramatic circumstances. (Above right) King Manuel visiting France with the President of the French Republic, Monsieur Loubet.

King Manuel was deposed by a republican revolution. He spent the rest of his life in exile in England, where he married Princess Augusta Victoria of Hohenzollern-Sigmaringen. (From left to right) The Prince of Wales (later Duke of Windsor), the Duke of Aosta, the Dowager Grand Duchess of Baden, unknown, Queen Amélie, her sister Hélène, Duchess of Aosta, the bride and bridegroom: behind them are the Crown Prince of Prussia, the King of Saxony and Infante Don Carlos.

Philippe, Duke of Orléans. Right: With his then fiancée and first cousin Princess Marguerite of Orléans. He suddenly broke the engagement to the fury of Marguerite's parents, the Duke and Duchess de Chartres.

Philippe, Duke of Orléans

His wife Archduchess Maria Dorothea of Austria, who was the granddaughter of Clementine of Orléans. As she could not have children she was not able to produce the expected heir. The marriage was very unhappy and ended in a separation.
Later Maria Dorothea lived on her properties in Hungary.

Philippe, Duke of Orleans, driving his car on his estate of Wood Norton, near London. Exiled from France, he lived in England but preferred to travel round the world. He went for long expeditions on his yacht the Maroussia, exploring the coasts of Greenland, Siberia and the Arctic. Unable to live in his own country, he could find rest nowhere.

The mother of Philippe, Duke of Orléans, the widowed Countess of Paris

50

Above: Four of the children of the Count and Countess of Paris, Princess Hélène, Princess Louise, Prince Ferdinand and Princess Isabelle. (Right) Princess Louise, who later married Prince Carlos of The Two Sicilies, Infante of Spain.

Left: Two of the sisters of the Duke of Orléans: Princess Hélène (left), who was briefly engaged to the Duke of Clarence, elder son of the future Edward VII, and Princess Isabelle.

The Countess of Paris with her grown up children, Princess Isabelle, Princess Hélène, Queen Amélie, the Duke of Montpensier, the Duke of Orléans and Princess Louise.

Princess Hélène with her husband Emmanuele of Savoy, Duke of Aosta, and their two sons, Amedeo and Aimone.

Princess Hélène (right) was a great beauty with a strong personality. She was also fearless and daring. A few years after her unhappy betrothal to the Duke of Clarence (above left) she married Emmanuele Filiberto of Savoy-Aosta, Duke of Aosta (above right). A general during the First World War, he won many battles while Hélène was renowned for her constant visits to the front and for organizing hospitals for the wounded. Like many members of the Orléans family, she loved far-away expeditions and embarked on long voyages through Africa

54

Left: From her trips, she also brought back a young black boy (above) whom she had bought on the slave market. She was furious when her elder sister Queen Amélie of Portugal had him christened. She was also a keen photographer and brought back fabulous photos of the African wilderness at the turn of the century. Right: The Aosta family at the end of the Second World War. In the middle, the old duchess Hélène; left, Duchess Anne with her daughter Marguerita and Duchess Irene, born a princess of Greece, with the second daughter of Duchess Anne, Princess Maria Christina. The young boy is the son of Duchess Irene, Amedeo, the present Duke of Aosta.

56

The Duke of Aosta, decorating his son during the war.

Far left: The Duke of Aosta's father had been made King of Spain for a few years, during the troubled period after Queen Isabelle II's exile, but this did not prevent Emmanuele Filiberto from receiving the lawful king of Spain, Alfonso XIII. From left to right: Queen Victoria Eugenia of Spain; the Duke of Aosta; King Alfonso XIII; Hélène, Duchess of Aosta and her second son Aimone, Duke of Spoleto.

Left: The Duke of Aosta and his cousin King Vittorio Emmanuele III at the christening of Princess Marguerita of Savoy-Aosta.

The youngest brother of Hélène, Duchess of Aosta, Ferdinand of France, Duke of Montpensier, married a young Spanish aristocrat with a large fortune, Isabella de Valdeterrasso. The wedding took place in the Château of Randan in Auvergne, which belonged to the Orléans family since the time of Louis Philippe.

58

The youngest daughter of the Count of Paris, Princess Louise, married Prince Carlos of the Two Sicilies, widow of the Princess of Asturias, the elder sister of King Alfonso XIII of Spain. The wedding took place at Wood Norton, the English residence of Princess Louise's brother the Duke of Orleans. The bride and bridegroom (left). The head of the Spanish royal family, King Alfonso XIII was present (far left), followed by the Duke of Montpensier. Many distinguished guests attended the wedding. Among them were Princess Louise of Coburg, born a princess of Belgium, with Infante Alfonso of Orléans and Bourbon (above left), The Duchess of Chartres, aunt of the bride, with the Prince of Bourbon-Two-Sicilies (above centre) and Queen Amélie of Portugal, eldest sister of the bride, with the Duke of Calabria, head of the royal house of Naples.

60

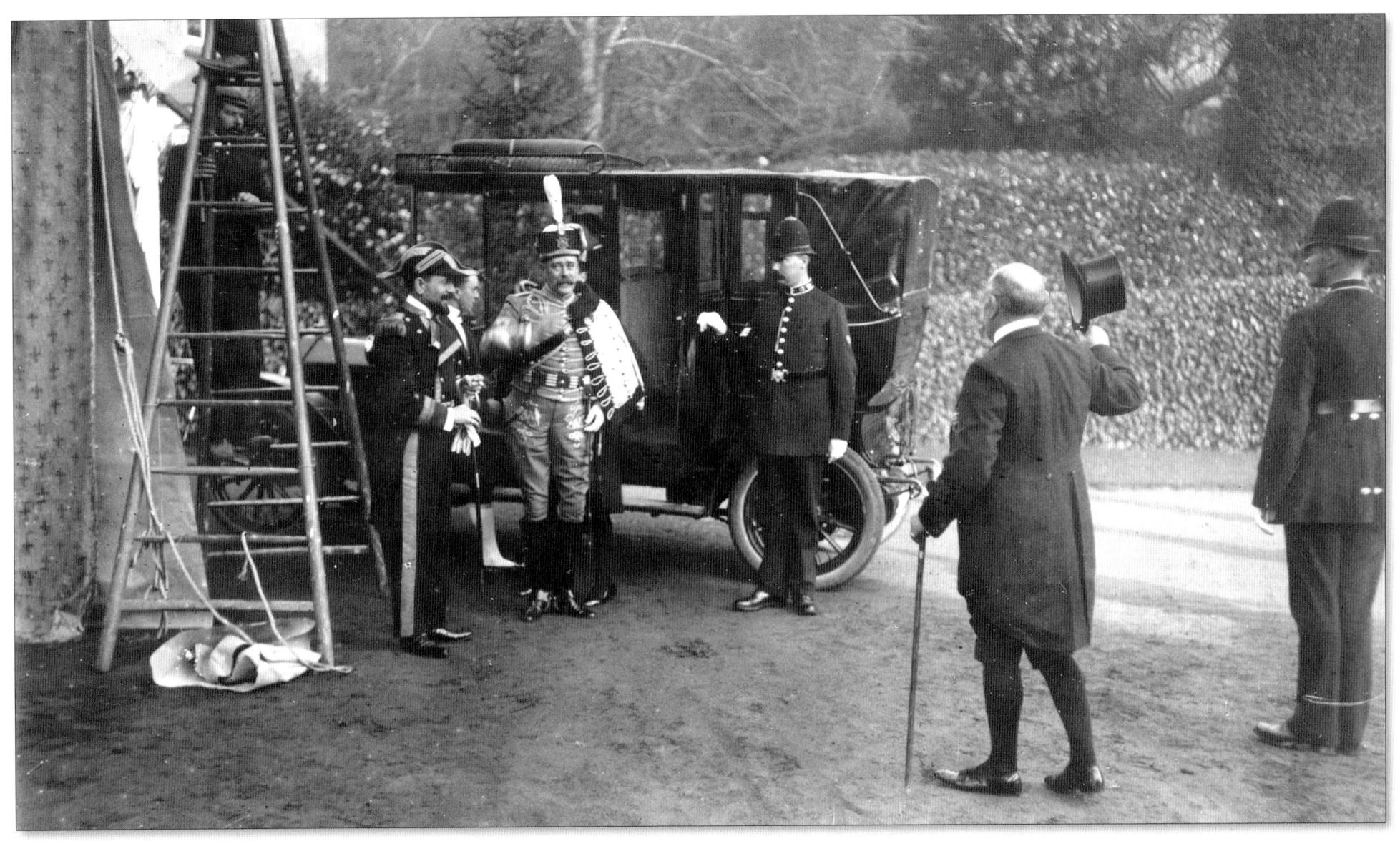

Above: Wood Norton, England. The bridegroom, Prince Carlos of the Two Sicilies, arrives for his wedding and is received by one of the gentlemen in attendance of the Duke of Orleans. Prince Carlos had a curious life. If Alfonso XIII had been a girl and if his first wife, the Princess of Asturias, had lived, she would have been Queen of Spain and he would have been Prince Consort. Fate avenged his disappointment when one of his daughters by his second marriage to princess Louise, Princess Maria de las Mercedes married Don Juan, Count of Barcelona, the heir to the Spanish throne. In due course Prince Carlos' grandson, Juan Carlos, became King of Spain.
Left: Wood Norton had been decorated with draperies bearing the symbol of the French royal house, the fleur de lys. In a corner, hidden by some A.D.C's, it is probably the King of Spain, taking the opportunity to smoke a cigarette unseen.

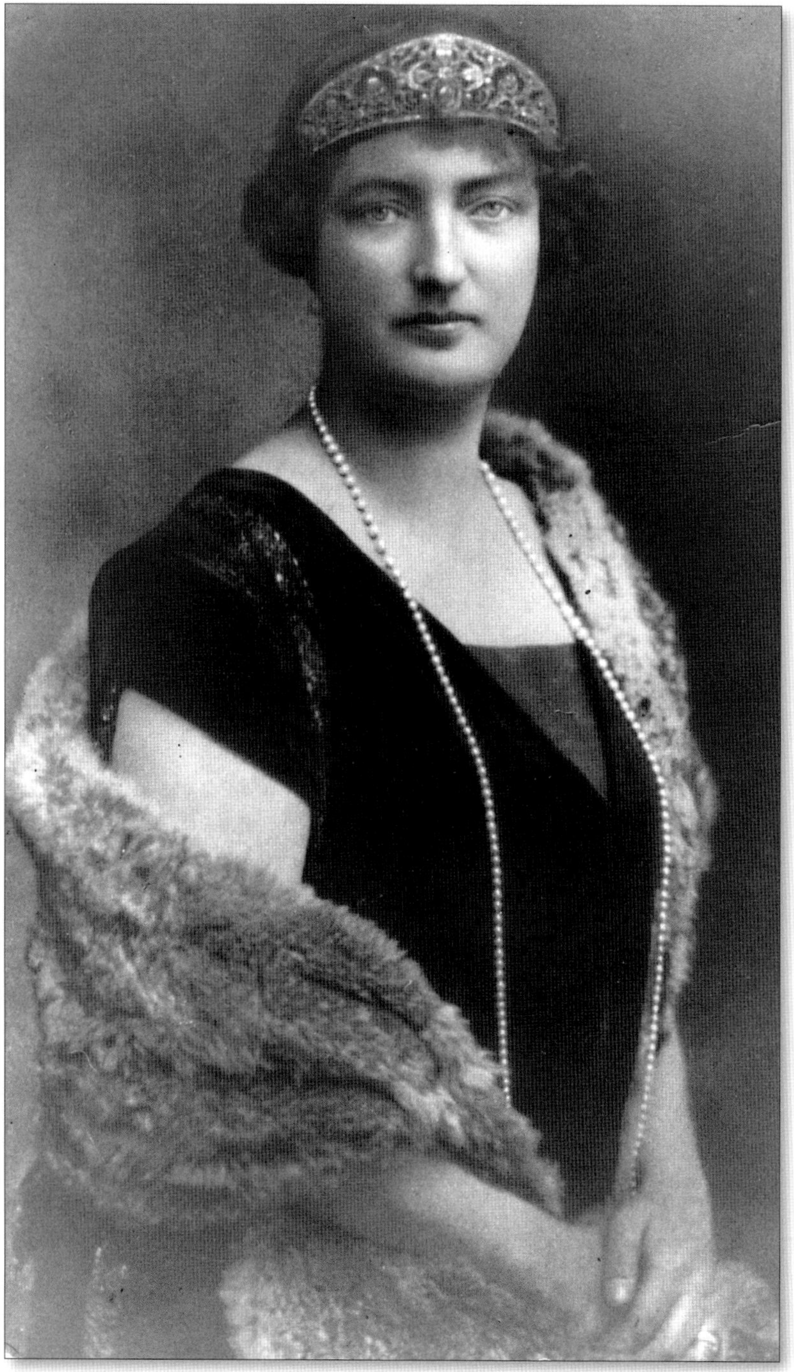

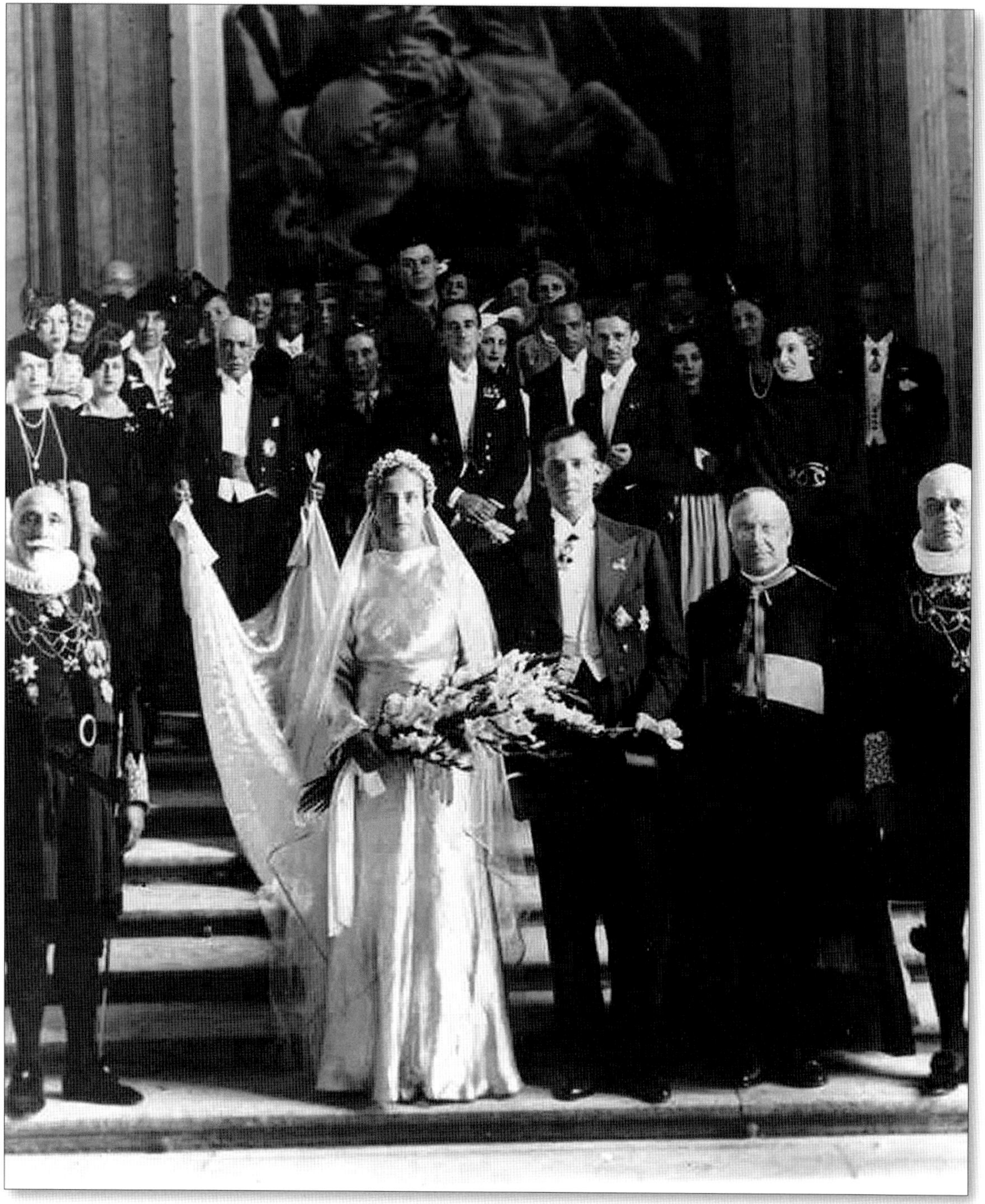

The French princes were denied by the republic the right to serve in the French army and to fight for their country. So, they found a cause to fight for in the American Civil War, serving gallantly in the northern armies. Above: Robert of Orleans, Duke of Chartres beside his elder brother Philippe, Count of Paris. First on the right is their uncle François of Orléans, Prince of Joinville. A few years later, the Duke of Chartres (right), found a way to defend his own country. The Franco-Prussian war of 1870 was raging and he managed to volunteer under the surname Le Fort, meaning 'the strong one'. It was the nickname of a distant ancestor in the 8th century.

Far left: Princess Louise of France, Infanta of Spain. Left: The wedding in Rome of Don Juan, Count of Barcelona, heir to King Alfonso XIII, and Princess Maria de las Mercedes, daughter of Prince Carlos of the Two Sicilies and Princess Louise. They had four children, among them, the present King of Spain.

64

Robert, Duke of Chartres, with his elder daughter, Marie of Orléans, who married Prince Waldemar of Denmark. Right: Two of the children of the Duke and Duchess of Chartres, Marie of Orléans and her younger brother, Jean of Orléans.

Far left: Another photograph of Robert of Orléans in uniform. He was also a keen photographer and took the oval picture of his wife Françoise of Orléans, Duchesse of Chartres, and their two daughters Marguerite and Marie. Below left: Françoise of Orléans, Duchess of Chartres, daughter of the Prince of Joinville. Below right: Their younger daughter, Marguerite of Orléans. After her brief engagement to her first cousin Philippe, Duke of Orléans, she married the son of the first president of the third republic, the 2nd Duke of Magenta. In her descendants, royal and republican blood is mixed.

The marriage of Marie d'Orléans to Valdemar of Denmark, the youngest son of King Christian IX, brought the French Royal family into contact with royalty from across the world. Princess Marie was sister-in-law to a Queen of Great Britain, an Empress of Russia and a King of Greece. In the first row, from left to right, are Prince George of Greece, Alexandra, the Princess of Wales, King Christian IX of Denmark, the Dowager Empress Marie of Russia, Tsar Nicholas II, King George I of Greece, Crown Princess Louise of Denmark, Queen Louise of Denmark, Crown Prince Frederick of Denmark, Princess Victoria of Great Britain, Empress Alexandra of Russia and Grand Duke Michael of Russia. Back row: Prince Christian (X), Princess Thyra, Prince Waldemar, Princess Marie, Prince Hans (brother of King Christian IX) and Princess Ingeborg.

Marie of Orléans married Prince Waldemar of Denmark, youngest son of King Christian IX. She was a very modern princess, one of the first to use the telephone, as seen in the picture (right). She was the honorary patron of the Copenhagen fire brigade and at every fire in the capital she would change her tiara for the fireman's helmet and run to do her duty. She was also an extraordinarily gifted artist and painter; many of her animal drawings were turned into figurines by the Royal Danish porcelain company. Above: Her husband Prince Waldemar of Denmark with four of their children, Axel, Erik, Viggo and Margrethe.

Prince Henri of Orléans, eldest son of the Duke of Chartres, was extremely gifted. Not only was he very handsome and a great success with the ladies, he was also a first-class explorer. His travel diaries are still essential reading for anyone who wishes to travel in Central Asia.

Prince Henri with his friend, a French explorer, with whom he explored the heart of the Asiatic continent.

Prince Henri died very young of yellow fever in Saigon. His body was brought back to France and buried in the family pantheon, the chapel of Dreux.

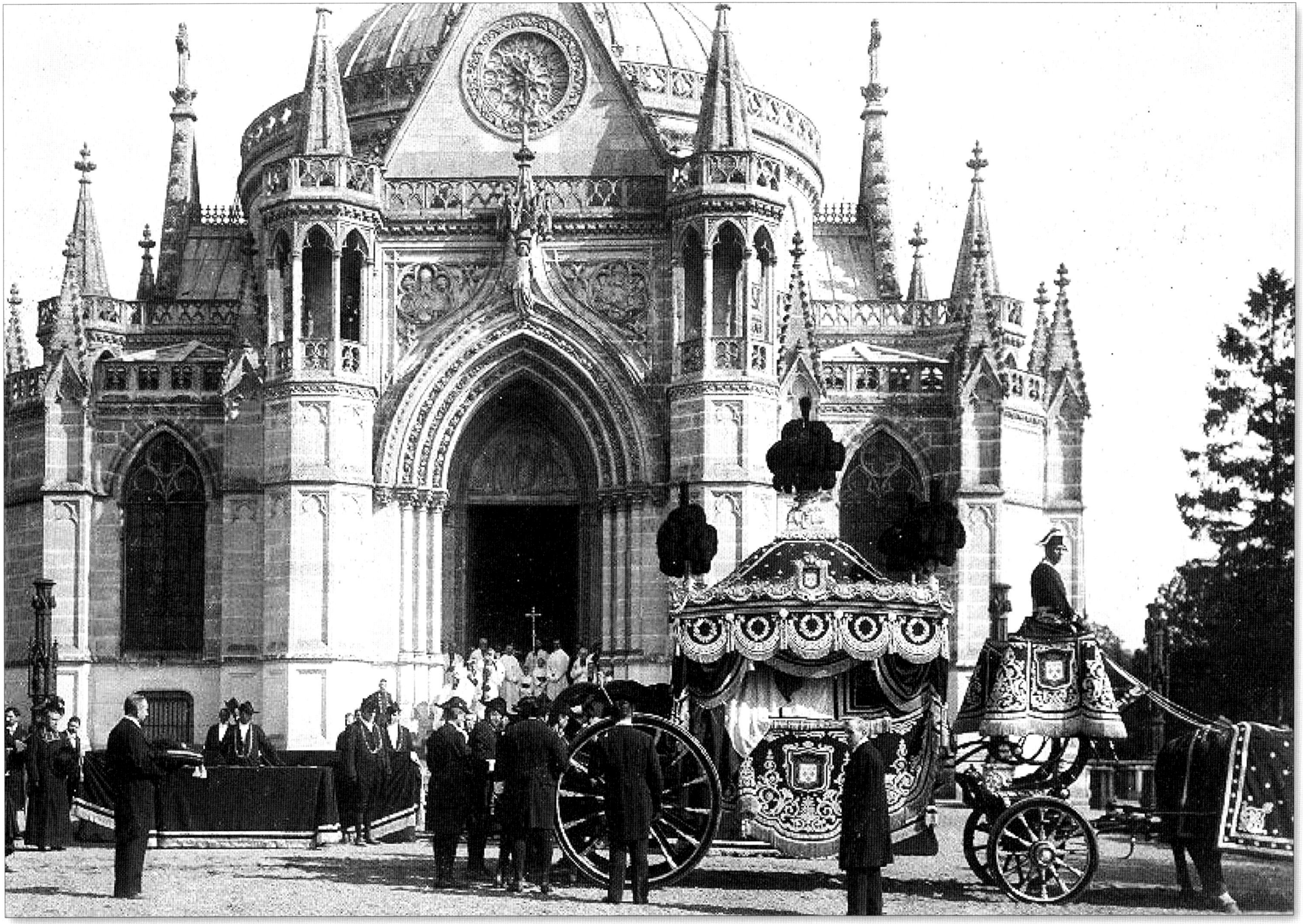

Jean of Orleans, Duke of Guise in Danish uniform. Prevented from serving in the French army, the Duke of Guise entered the Danish army thanks to his sister, Princess Marie who was a daughter-in-law of King Christian IX. During the First World War, the Duke of Guise also managed to serve as a stretcher-bearer. He loved Paris and his military collections and nothing made him happier than to explore the "bouquinistes" along the Seine. Following the deaths of other male members of the Orléans family, Jean of Orléans one day found himself head of the French Royal House. To his utter despair, he was then forced immediately into exile from France, .

Three pictures of Princess Isabelle, the third daughter of the Count of Paris, and by far the most beautiful member of the family. She married her first cousin Jean of Orléans, Duke of Guise. Bored with her life in northern France, in a sinister castle called Le Nouvion, she took her husband and four children to Morocco, which was then a wild country. She settled there and was given lands, which the family farmed, and they lived there blissfully happy until the Duke and Duchess of Guise were forced to return to Europe.

The Duke and Duchess of Chartres in old age. They lived in the little château of Saint Firmin in the huge domain of Chantilly, which belonged to their uncle the Duke of Aumale. Not in exile like his brother, the Count of Paris and his nephew the Duke of Orléans, the Duke of Chartres could live in France but he had to cooperate with the regime, so his nephews accused him of being republican. On the photograph to the right are two of their grandchildren, Princesses Isabelle and Françoise of Orléans, daughters of the Duke and Duchess of Guise. The Duke's great entertainment in Chantilly was hunting and he had his own pack of hounds.

Jean of Orléans, Duke of Guise, preferred a very simple life. Here he is at the beach with his second daughter, Princess Françoise.

His mother the Duchess of Chartres was far more grand. Here, she is riding with the Chantilly hunt. Like her father the Prince of Joinville, the Duchess of Chartres was a remarkable artist. Among other things, she left a collection of more than 300 watercolours representing every conceivable kind of mushroom.

Left: At a hunting party in Chantilly, the Duchess of Chartres wearing a bowler hat. With her is her niece and daughter-in-law Isabelle, Duchess of Guise, who did not like her at all: also her two granddaughters, Princesses Isabelle and Françoise of Orléans. The Duchess of Guise did not enjoy staying at Saint Firmin with her in-laws, she much preferred Andalucia and Spain, the country of her mother the Countess of Paris. She was never more happy than when riding in the feria of Seville with her sister, the Infanta Louise (above).

Isabelle of France, Duchess of Guise at the time of her marriage to her first cousin Jean of Orléans.

After her husband became head of the House of France and pretender to the throne, she is wearing the parure of sapphires and diamonds said to have belonged to Marie Antoinette, which her mother the Countess of Paris wore before her.

When, in 1925, Jean of Orléans, Duke of Guise became head of the House of France, he and his wife divided their time between Europe, as close as they could be to France, from whom the duc de Guise was exiled, and Morocco, a home the Duchess of Guise was refusing to give up. Above: First communion in Morocco, with a rather rustic setting, for the two youngest children of the Duke of Guise, Princess Anne and Prince Henri, the future Count of Paris.

The Duke of Guise was exiled but the Duchess of Guise could return to France. So, on the death of her brother the Duke of Orléans, she hosted a solemn requiem in the Cathedral of Notre-Dame in Paris which, for the first time in centuries, saw the fleur-de-lis on its walls. Above left: Inside the Cathedral. Below left: Leaving the Cathedral: the Duchess of Guise followed on the left by her daughter, Princess Françoise.

Right: The House of France shortly after the Duke of Guise became head of the family: Sitting, left to right: the Count of Paris, the Duchess and the Duke of Guise. Standing: Count Bruno d'Harcourt, Princesses Françoise, Anne, and Isabelle of Orléans,

77

Princess Isabelle, the eldest daughter of the Duke and Duchesse of Guise was first married to Count Bruno d'Harcourt with whom she had four children (left), Bernard, Gilone, Isabelle and Monique. After the accidental death of her husband, she remarried Prince Pierre Murat, descendant of one of the Napoleon's generals who had married the Emperor's sister Caroline (above).

Henri, Count of Paris, son of the Duke of Guise. Early on, the Count's involvement in politics distanced him from the very powerful French royalist party, l'Action Française, which he found too extreme in its right-wing views.

Princess Françoise, beloved sister of the Count of Paris, photographed in the gardens of the Anastasia Villa, her Roman residence. The photograph was taken by Hoyningen Huene.

The Duchess of Guise and her sister, the Duchess of Aosta, planned the wedding of their children, Anne of France and Amedeo of Aosta. The ceremony took place with all the necessary pomp and circumstance in Naples, where Hélène, the Dowager Duchess of Aosta was living. Above: The bridal procession crossing the square that separates the church where the ceremony took place from the royal palace of Naples.

Right: Very quickly after their wedding the young couple, who bore the titles Duke and Duchess of Pouilles, took part in a historical tournament in Turin. Amedeo of Aosta took the part of his ancestor Duke Victor Amedeo, and Anne of the Duke's wife, the famous Madame Royale Christine de France, sister of Louis XIII.

81

Amedeo of Savoy-Aosta, Duke of Pouilles, was an adventurer, a marvellous soldier, a charming man and by far the most popular member of the Italian royal family. He served in Libya where he did not hesitate to explore the desert (left). A highly skilled pilot, he is photgraphed at the helm of a small plane with his wife Anne and their eldest daughter Marguerita behind him (above).

Once the couple became Duke and Duchess of Aosta, they were offered the famous castle of Miramare, built by Emperor Maximilian of Mexico, as their residence. They were the last to live in the castle before it became the property of the Italian republic. Right: Princess Marguerita of Savoy-Aosta in a Tahitian costume. running on the terrace of Miramare. Far right: The Duke of Aosta was particularly fond of his first cousin and sister-in-law Princess Françoise.

83

Princess Françoise of France, second daughter of the Duke of Guise, became engaged in 1928 to Prince Christopher of Greece, the youngest son of King George I and Grand Duchess Olga of Russia. At the time he was living in exile in Rome and Françoise's aunt, the Dowager Duchess Hélène, brought the two of them together. They became engaged at the palace of Capodimonte, her residence.

Princess Françoise was renowned for her beauty as well as for her kindness. Above she is wearing a gift from her husband, a turquoise and diamond ornament created by Fabergé. Right: Posing for Vogue magazine.

Princess Françoise and Prince Christopher at the time of their engagement, in front of the palace of Capodimonte

Once settled in Rome, Princess Françoise was reunited with the uncle she had known since childhood, King Alfonso XIII of Spain, who was in exile in the Italian capital

Prince Christopher and Princess Françoise during a picnic

Princess Françoise and her father the Duke of Guise moving towards the Palatine Chapel of the palace of the Norman Kings.

The bride and groom signing the matrimonial act; behind them is the Count of Paris, brother of the bride.

The wedding of Princess Françoise and Prince Christopher of Greece in Palermo in February 1929. The bride and groom during the ceremony

Prince Christopher about to go on honeymoon at the wheel of his splendid Rolls Royce.

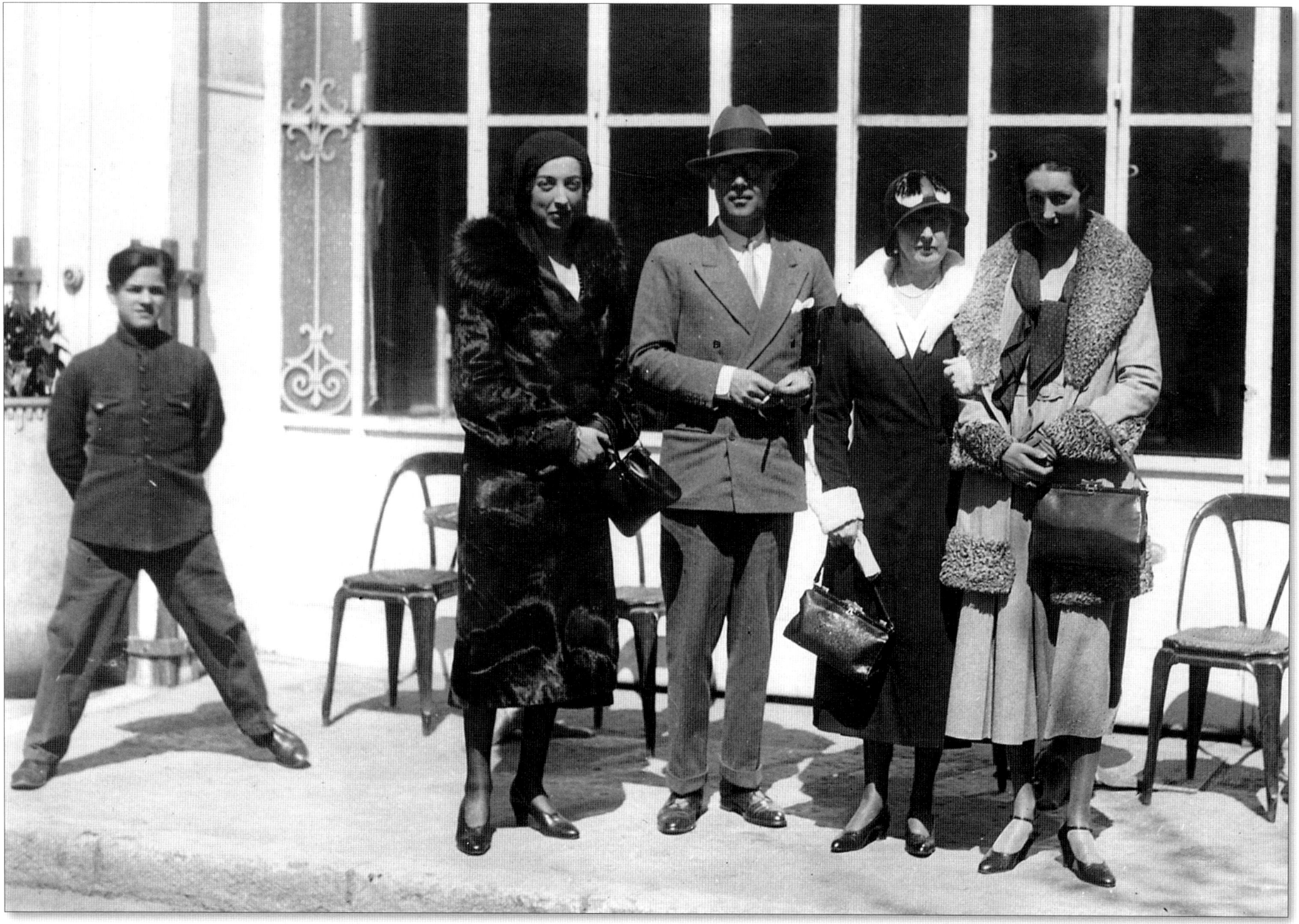

Prince Christopher, who was a member of the Orthodox Church, accompanies his wife to Sunday mass in a Catholic church in Rome, Saint Louis of France, which was Princess Françoise' favourite.

Right: Princess Françoise and Prince Christopher in the garden of the Anastasia villa, their Roman residence.

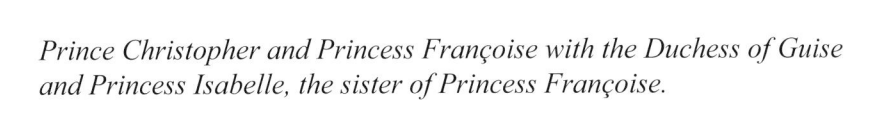

Prince Christopher and Princess Françoise with the Duchess of Guise and Princess Isabelle, the sister of Princess Françoise.

The Count of Paris, son and heir of the Duke of Guise, married Princess Isabelle of Orléans-Braganza in Palermo. Here, the Count of Paris is holding the arm of his mother the Duchess of Guise, followed by the Duke of Guise arm-in-arm with Queen Amélie of Portugal, leaving the palace of the Norman Kings and moving towards the cathedral in Palermo where the bridal ceremony was to take place.

Above right:
The Count and Countess of Paris during the bridal ceremony

Below right:
The young bride and groom greeting the crowd of French royalists from the balcony of the Orléans palace

Far right:
In the gardens of the Orléans palace during the reception of the royalists: the Duke and Duchess of Guise on either side of their daughter, Princess Françoise.

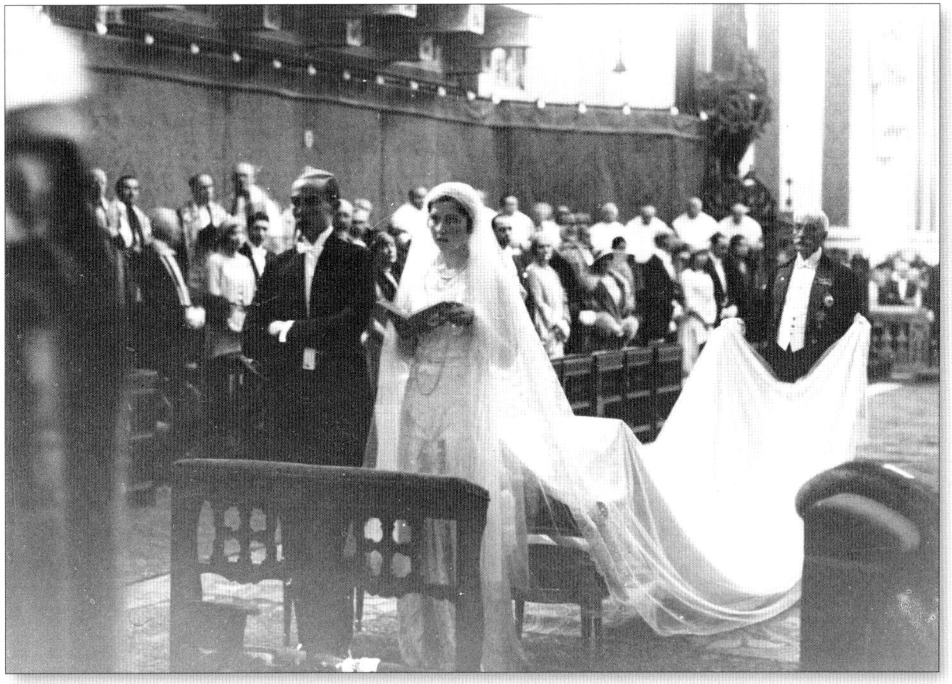

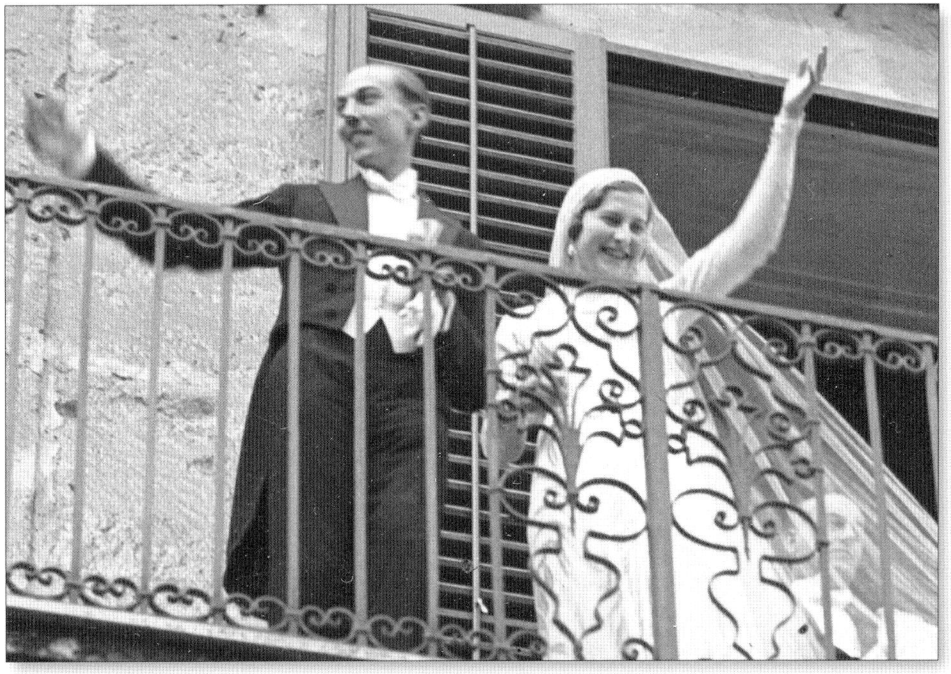

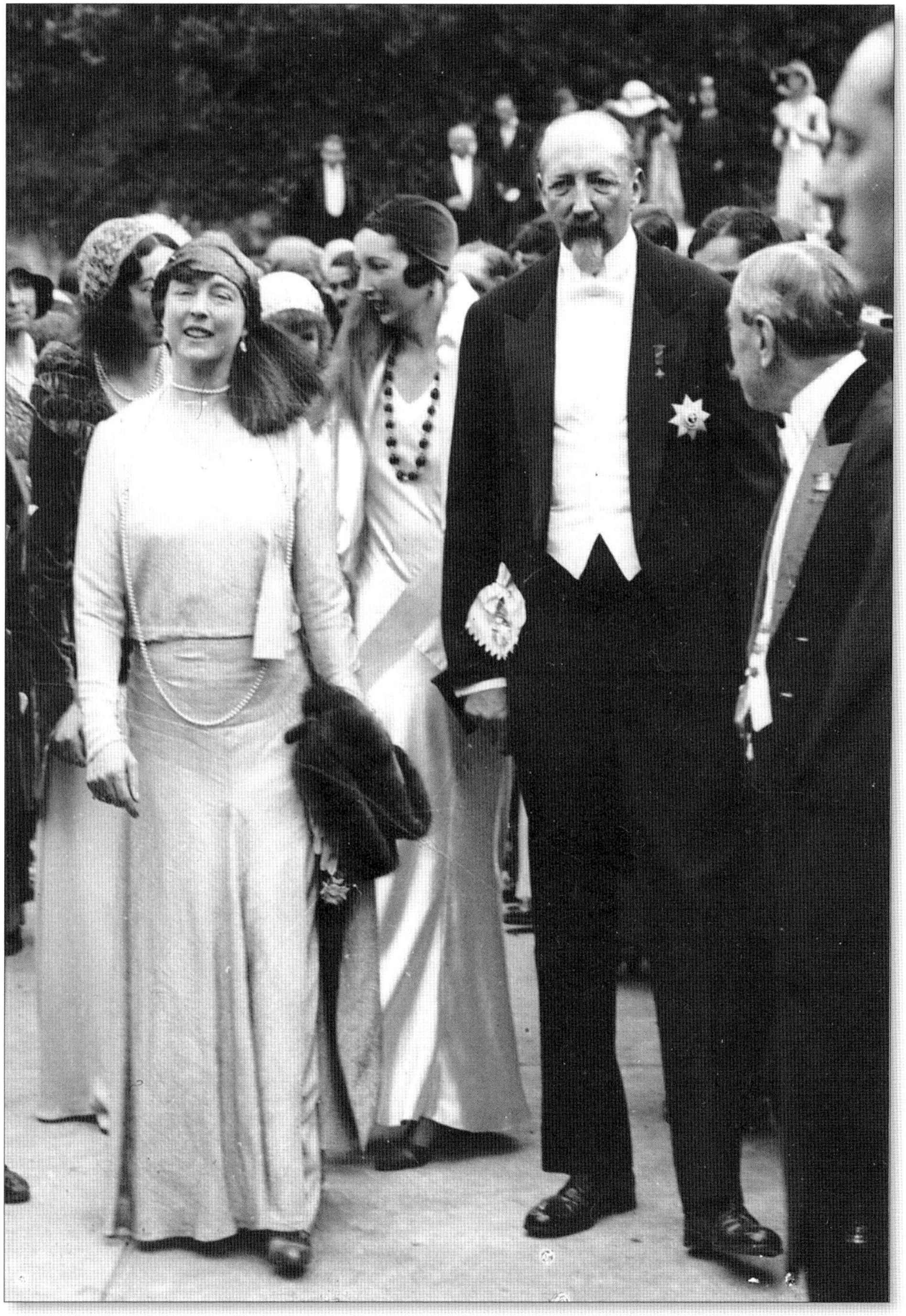

*The Duke and Duchess of Guise and their son the Count of Paris paying a visit to the Pope at the Vatican.
At this time serious disagreements had opened a gulf between the French royalist party, l'Action Française,
and the Catholic church and it took all the diplomacy of the House of France to restore their ties during this visit.*

Because of his exile the Duke of Guise saw his political influence weaken. His wife, on the other hand, would make trips to France which had all the flavour of an election campaign. Beautiful, intelligent and majestic, with a flame burning in her heart, she won over anyone who approached her and attracted crowds. People would shout "Long live the Queen" with such enthusiasm that it worried the republic. Above: The Duchess of Guise wearing the famous 'Marie Antoinette' sapphires and diamonds. Right: The Duke and Duchess of Guise sitting in the hall of a hotel in Brussels where they were living at the time.

Princess Françoise and Prince Christopher with their only child Michael, born in January 1939 - me!

Note on the Titles of the House of France

The children of the head of the House of France are Princes or Princesses of France and also Princes or Princesses of Orléans. Other members of the Royal House are simply Princes or Princesses of Orléans.

William Mead Lalor
ROYALTY BEFORE THE WARS
2003, 96 pages, 180 ill. large format
ISBN 91-973978-5-7 This collection covers "The Golden Age of Royalty", the period between the turn of the century and up to the first World War. Splendid formal portraits along with large family groups, and with the emphasis on the minor Royal and Princely families of Europe.
SEK 280

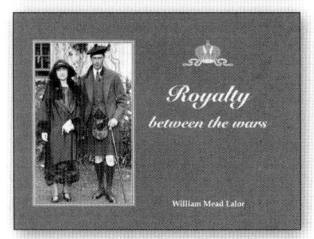

William Mead Lalor
ROYALTY BETWEEN THE WARS
2005, 96 pages, 136 ill. large format
ISBN 91-630-8284-5
Volume two in this series deals mostly with the 20s and 30s. The majority of Royal Families had seized to reign and in many cases gone into exile. A truly unique collection of a hard-to-find pictorial documentation.
SEK 280

William Mead Lalor
ROYALTY AFTER THE WARS
2001, 96 pages, 159 ill. large format
ISBN 91-973978-2-2 The third volume in this series deals with the period from the end of World War II up until around 1970. A difficult period for the collector of Royal pictures, but the author has a truly unique collection, from which it was possible to put together this most enjoyable album.
SEK 280

HM KING MICHAEL I OF ROMANIA
[SM Le Roi Michel Ier de Romanie]
A Tribute - Un Hommage
[in English and French] ISBN 91-973978-3-0
2001, 96 pages, 113 b/w and 25 colour ill.
King Michael - his life in pictures, with text by his daughter and son-in-law. A unique life, a unique book! Dedications by the King of Spain and by the Prince of Wales. Pictures from the private albums of the Romanian Royal Family.
SEK 360

Robert Golden
RELATIVELY ROYAL
A personal view
2000, 96 pages, 140 ill. large format.
ISBN 91-973978-1-4 **SEK 280**

Two glorious photo albums, covering the extended family of Queen Victoria, including the Battenbergs, the Fifes, the Cambridges, the Connaughts, the Harewoods, the Athlones and many others. Entertaining text by an author who actually knew many of these Royals and semi-Royals personally.

Robert Golden
THE GOLDEN BOOK OF ROYALTY
Relatively speaking
2002, 96 pages, 160 ill. large format.
ISBN 91-973978-5-7 **SEK 280**

David McIntosh
DIE UNBEKANNTEN HABSBURGER
THE UNKNOWN HABSBURGS
2000, 96 pages, 120 ill. [in English & German]
A unique collection of pictures and pedigrees of the Tuscany (Toscana) branch of the Habsburg dynasty. Leopold Wölfling, the Crown Princess of Saxony and Johann Orth - they are all there. Pedigrees included. **SEK 280**

David McIntosh
THE GRAND DUKES OF OLDENBURG
2007, 88 pages, 190 ill. large format
ISBN 91-975671-3-2 The history, genealogy and iconography of a small German Grand Duchy and its ruling family. The Oldenburgs were connected to the dynasties of almost every country in Europe, including Denmark, Sweden, Russia, Prussia, Bavaria and Mecklenburg. **SEK 280**

Antoinette Ramsay Herthelius - Ted Rosvall
ASTRID 1905 – 1935
2005, 80 pages, 106 ill. large format ISBN 91-975671-0-8 A memorial album focusing the legendary Queen Astrid of the Belgians, Princess of Sweden. Published in connection with the centenary of her birth, this unique album includes pictures from her childhood, youth, marriage and short time as Crown Princess and Queen. Text in Swedish & English. **SEK 280**

David William Cripps
ROYAL CABINET PORTRAITS
of the Victorian Era
2003, 96 pages, 190 ill. large format
ISBN 91-973978-6-5. A new Royal Picture Album, focusing Queen Victoria's children, grandchildren, great grandchildren and other close relatives. Many unique portraits from the Courts of Russia, Prussia, Hesse and from other Royal families. **SEK 280**

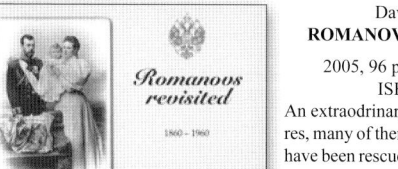

David William Cripps
ROMANOVS REVISITED 1860-1960
2005, 96 pages, 212 ill. large format
ISBN 91-975671-1-6
An extraodrinary collection of Romanov pictures, many of them never before published. Some have been rescued from old and partly destroyed glass-plates. Splendour and grandeur but also intimate snapshots. **SEK 280**

Diana Mandache
Marie of Romania
Images from a Royal Life
2007, 96 pages, 210 ill. [in English]
The life and times of a romantic and legendary Queen and her family. Marie of Edinburgh, Queen Victoria's granddaughter, became Queen of Romania and the mother-in-law of the Balkans. Unique illustrations. **SEK 280**

Subscribe to **ROYALTY DIGEST Quarterly**

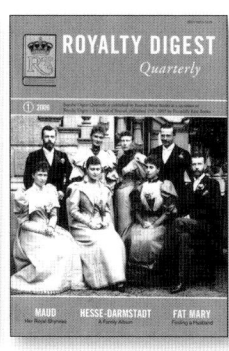

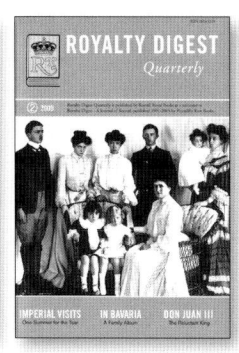

An in-depth royalty magazine, now in its 5th year, focusing the lesser known royal families of Europe. Each issue has 64 pages and over 100 illustrations. Family albums, genealogies, biographies, royal portraits, book reviews, royal news - and more. Subscriptions are SEK 400 [ca £ 32] per year. VISA, Mastercard and IBAN accepted. All back issues still available.

royalbooks@telia.com   tel 0046-515-37105

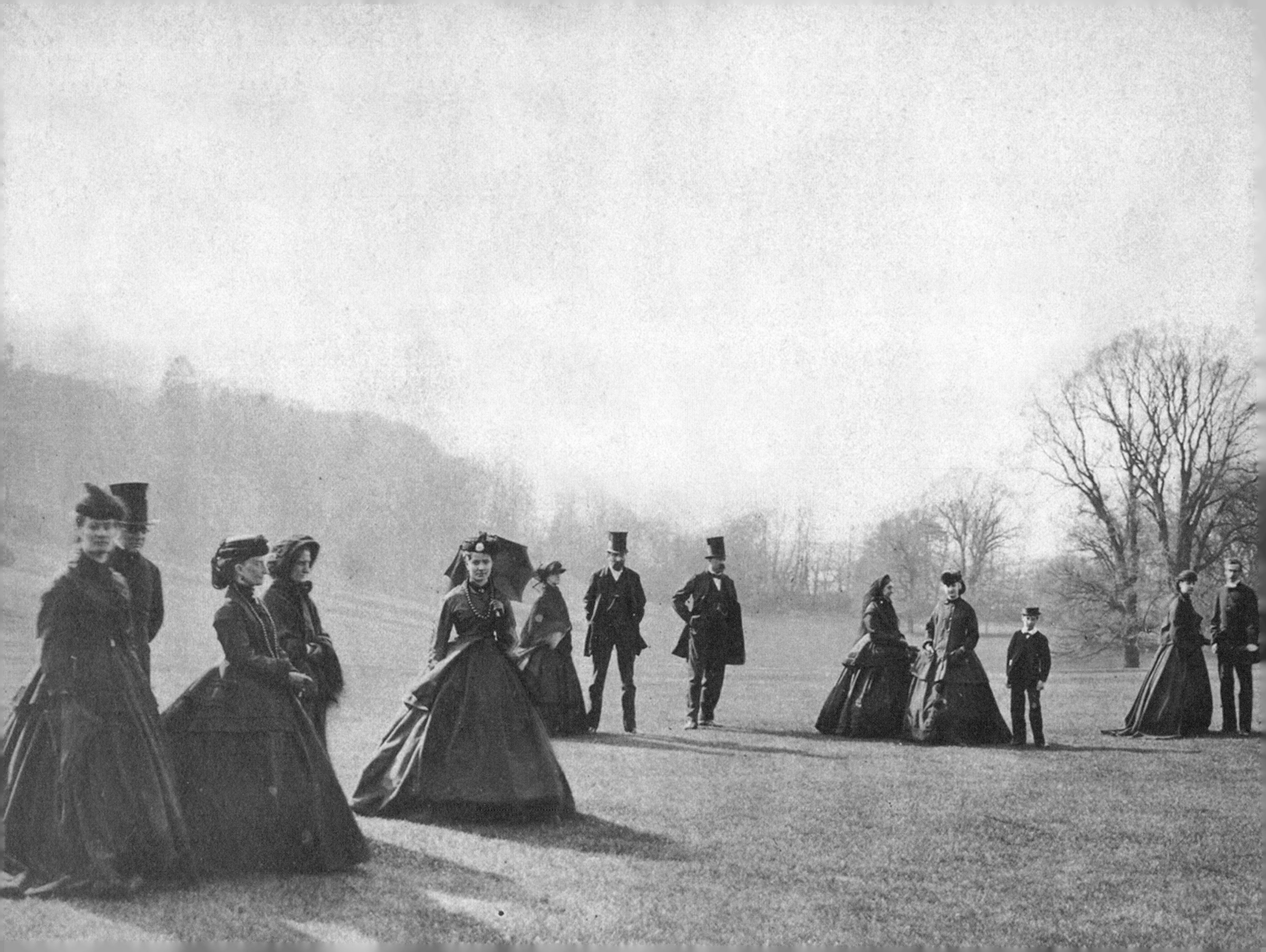